Letting God Sort It

ML Stone

CF4•K

Copyright © M L Stone 2017

10 9 8 7 6 5 4 3 2 1

Paperback ISBN: 978-1-5271-0046-6

e-pub ISBN: 978-1-5271-0085-5

mobi ISBN: 978-1-5271-0086-2

First published in 2017 by

Christian Focus Publications Ltd,

Geanies House, Fearn, Ross-shire

IV20 1TW, Scotland

www.christianfocus.com

Cover and internal graphics by Pete Barnsley (Creativehoot.com)

Printed and bound by Bell and Bain, Glasgow

Scripture taken from the Contemporary English Version © 1991, 1992, 1995 by American Bible Society, Used by permission.

Scripture quotations [marked ESV] taken from the Holy Bible, English Standard Version, published by HarperCollinsPublishers © 2001 by Crossway Bibles, a division of Good News Publishers. Used by permission. All rights reserved.

Scripture quotations [marked NIV] taken from the Holy Bible, New International Version Anglicised © 2004 Biblica. Used by permission of Hodder & Stoughton Ltd, an Hachette UK company. All rights reserved. 'NIV' is a registered trademark of Biblica UK trademark number 1448790.

CONTENTS

Introduction 9

#thecreativecreatorcreates 11

#itsuptoyou 13

#holyisthelordGodalmighty 15

#yessir 17

#hewilldoit 19

#promisekeeper 21

#ringring 23

#aintnomountain 25

#goodgifts 27

#examtime 29

#thatsmine 31

#sweetdreams 33

#icanseeyou 35

#onmyown 37

#whatstheplan 39

#whoseplanisitanyway 41

#actiontime 43

#themasterplan 45

#thearrival 47

#theteenageyears 49

#thecousin 51

#thedesert 53

#whoyouare 55

#nocrustsplease 57

#lightoflife...59

#whatsnewwithewe...61

#feelingsheepish 63

#lifeparttwo...65

#threeforthepriceofone.....................................67

#grapeplant..69

#mountainshoutin 71

#itsnotaboutthemoney.......................................73

#workingninetofive 75

#rumblingtummies...77

#waterwalker...79

#Lazarusraised 81

#thelittledudes 83

#storytime...85

#justkeepswimming..87

#thegoodthebadandtheugly 89

#finderskeepers 91

#branchingout 93

#smellysocks...95

#suppertime..97

#endingsandbeginnings......................................99

#itstoolate 101

#daythree 103

#intrusionofconfusion......................................105

#nowyouseehim 107

Dedication

For Chris, who first gave me an opportunity to write, and took time to encourage me when she wasn't driving up and down the A9.

For Izzy, whose help on this project (as well as the constant supply of fresh hen eggs) has been invaluable.

For Dad, who has helped me with my many questions on both biblical and motorcycle-related topics.

INTRODUCTION

I love a life hack. A little method to make life a bit happier, a snippet of wisdom to get the job done a tad faster, or a clever trick to make my day go just a smidgen more smoothly.

Jump online and you can find thousands of life hacks from people all across the world, each purporting to have that special piece of wisdom to help you to 'do life' more effectively.

But who has the right answers? Who has the real know-how? Where can you turn for the ultimate guide on how to live life?

(Can you see where I'm going here?)

Who better to look to for some advice on living than the life-maker Himself!?!

Long before the creation of the internet, God shared with mankind (through His Word) all we need to know about who He is, His mission to this world, and how He wants us to live.

This fifty day Bible reading challenge will take us through different parts of the Bible, looking at what God has told us about Himself, and how He guides us to live.

The creator of any invention is best-placed to put together the user instructions, and so we can have confidence that the 'life hacks' that God (our maker!) has given us in the Bible are trustworthy and worth paying attention to.

So let's dive in and get hacking!

#getready

#getreading

#thecreativecreatorcreates

READ GENESIS 1

I don't like to brag, but when I was only ten years old I won the school award for art. That's right. The Castletown Primary School Art Badge 1998. I received said badge because I drew a picture of our class hamster (imaginatively named 'Mr Hamster').

In retrospect, I can tell you with some certainty that that piece of art was 100% garbage, and had Mr Hamster been able to articulate his response to this portrait, it would have been far from positive!

I was, and still am, terrible at drawing and I really didn't deserve any recognition for my efforts.

Perhaps you are a bit more artistic than me, but how does your very best work of art compare to God's, given that He created the universe??

It's easy to skip through the first chapter of Genesis, easy to become used to the beauty and complexity of nature. But stop! Think! Imagine! God created this incredible, beautiful, awesome, complex world, and mankind itself, with just words. Wow! Mind blowing stuff!

If I was given a badge for my, frankly, horrible drawing of Mr Hamster, what should be given to honour the God who has created this majestic universe?

Well, the Bible tells us He deserves 'glory, honour and power' (Revelation 4:11). But how do we give Him that? With our words in prayer and when we sing to God in worship, and even in how we live our lives. We have a responsibility to protect, learn about and celebrate the created world, all in honour of this awesome Creator.

GOD FACT: God's power, creativity and awesomeness are off the scale!

LIFE HACK: Today, as you walk about in creation, keep your eyes open to amazing things God has made – big or small. Praise Him by telling Him what you think of what He's made.

#itsuptoyou

A friend took me fishing recently, which was something I hadn't done since childhood. She gave me all the relevant instructions and sent me around the pond from her. The last piece of advice she gave me was that I should keep the bait – some doomed maggots, heading for a soggy end – safely in the tin.

Attempting to get organised, I found the lid of the bait tin quite difficult to unscrew. I would struggle to open it every time I needed to get a maggot out. It seemed better to me to decant said maggots into my empty crisp packet and whip one out when I needed it.

All was going well, until ten minutes later when I went to get a new maggot. They were ALL gone. Every single one had escaped. Freedom had beckoned and they'd answered the call.

Something similar (although with far more serious and long lasting consequences!) is what we see happen with Adam and Eve. Someone who knew FAR better had told them how to live. Someone with authority, wisdom and love who had their best interests at heart. But Adam and Eve decided to ignore all this, to distrust God and to do what they thought was best.

Eve doesn't see what the problem really is! Underneath it all is the belief that she knows better than God – and that He is an untrustworthy liar. The consequences of their sin were devastating.

Not just for Adam and Eve, but for all mankind.

Think you know best? Think again! (And always keep your maggots in a tin).

GOD FACT: God gives free will. He doesn't force anyone to go His way, He gives us a choice.

LIFE HACK: Today if you are tempted to do or say something that you know is not God's way, remember the example of Adam and Eve. Will you choose to follow your own dodgy judgement? Or the command of an all-loving, all-knowing God, who can always be trusted.

#holyisthelordGodalmighty

READ GENESIS 6:5-22

The day will come when you will have to face a task that daunts many…. doing your own laundry. Well, let me share one of my top tips with you, passing on a piece of wisdom that my mother passed to me.

Don't put your red socks in with your white shirt. Trust me. Unless you want to have a blotchy pink shirt, akin to the colour of an old flamingo, then don't do it. Just don't. It doesn't take much to completely ruin a pristine white shirt. A red sock, a burst pen, your baby niece chundering her lunch on your shoulder…

In the same way, it didn't take much to ruin God's perfect world. In Genesis 6 we see just how sinful the world had become and just how sad this made God. But not just sad, He was (rightly) angry at what was going on. He was and is a holy and just God and that meant He had to act.

The story of the flood reminds us that God isn't our personal assistant or our pet. He's no Santa Claus or jolly grandfather figure. Whilst He might be our friend, He is also the holy, awesome and to be feared Yahweh. A God we couldn't even look on and survive (see Exodus 33:20). He is not a God we can simply put in our pocket. He is a God who rightly decrees that those who aren't holy will face judgement for their sin. The sins these people committed brought about their own destruction.

We don't have an ark to keep us safe. But don't worry, we have something better! We have a Jesus! And Jesus is superior to a wooden boat in practically every way. The ark kept those inside safe for a limited time, but Jesus ensures our safety and protection for eternity.

Jesus took all the wrath and destruction you deserve, in YOUR place. In return, you are given His holiness and are made acceptable to God. When God looks at you, He sees a righteous man or woman – much more righteous than Noah. You can now call God a friend, and not have any fear about facing His judgement in this world, or the next.

GOD FACT: God is holy, and sin cannot co-exist with Him. He is to be feared and respected. But Jesus took our punishment, making a way for us to be friends with God.

LIFE HACK: Pray that God would give you a better understanding of who He is and that you would grow in both your knowledge of His love for you, and your respect for His holiness.

#yessir

READ GENESIS 7:1-24

It's easy to follow an instruction that makes sense. But what about the ones that seem a bit left field? For example, if your mum told you to put on your wellies, when it was clearly a rainy day, you'd probably get those spotty bad-boys on a.s.a.p! But what if you were heading for a BBQ on a sunny summer day? You'd probably have something to say.

Noah got one of those weird instructions. God asked him to build an ark. In the middle of the desert.

You can imagine it might have been a bit of a struggle for Noah to do what he had been asked. An Ark? Had he heard God properly? Maybe he'd misheard…. maybe God had said build a greenhouse? A giant sand castle? A solar powered sun cream factory? Nah, He'd said an ark!

Although Noah's task must have been hard and confusing, we see in verse 5 that 'he did everything the Lord told him to do.' Everything. Every big and small instruction was followed. In the face of logic, in spite of mocking from his community, and at great cost to himself, Noah obeyed.

And what was the result? Following God's instructions meant that Noah saved himself, his family and a zoo's worth of animals!

Although it's unlikely that God will ask any of us to build an ark, some of His commands can seem hard to understand. But in both the short and long term, when we follow God's instructions it always works for our good – and for the good of God's Kingdom.

GOD FACT: God demands obedience. His ways are best and can be trusted.

LIFE HACK: Resolve to obey God's instructions today in the same way that Noah did. Not picking and choosing when we do and when we don't, but always going His way, even when it doesn't make sense to us.

#hewilldoit

Have you ever been stuck inside for too long? It's stormy outside, you're not feeling very well, or you're waiting for a package to be delivered ('any time between 7am and your 65th birthday').

It's not much fun. You end up feeling cooped up and can start to get irritated by other people in your space. 'Cabin fever' is apparently the official pirating term for such a condition!

Imagine you're holed up somewhere small. Then add your whole family into the mix. Then add a ton of animals. Then add a limited variety of food. Also bear in mind that there is restricted ventilation, deodorant hasn't been invented, and there are no flushing toilets (although not sure the animals would have made use of these even if they had been available….). You can't go outside and there's no escape from your family. It's hot, it's smelly, it's noisy and Ham snores more loudly than the elephants!

Minus the snoring, that was Noah's situation. It would have been very hard going for him and his family. BUT he knew there was a finish line ahead. He knew God had said it would rain for forty days and forty nights. And God did exactly what He had promised. The rain stopped just as He said it would.

Now, Noah and the gang still had to wait a long time before they could actually get off that ark, but as their food supplies dwindled and their water was rationed out, they trusted that God had promised their deliverance and that they could depend on His Word.

And, of course, He came through.

What would you have done the moment that ark door opened? A somersault? A short but moving dance routine? Perhaps grabbed a horse and ridden off into the sunset?

Noah did none of the above. Instead, he built an altar and gave a sacrifice of thanks to the God who had kept him, his family and a boatload of animals safe. (I mean, maybe he threw a high-kick in there too, we'll never know).

Noah's top priority was thanking the God who had delivered on what He had promised.

GOD FACT: God is faithful. If He has said something, He will do it. End of!

LIFE HACK: Endeavour to be like your heavenly Father. If you say something, make sure you do it! If you've made a commitment and not followed through, then make a plan today to rectify that. Follow up on your words with action, and trust that God will do the same.

#promisekeeper

E ver say something and then regret it? I was working at a camp recently where we'd all enjoyed some delicious chilli and a few of the team were getting on with the dishes. Time was short but they were confident they could get them done in the fifteen minutes before the evening meeting. I, however, wasn't so confident. 'Yeah, right,' I declared. 'If you get them done in 15 minutes, I'll eat a bowl of slops.'

Any guesses what I had for my supper that night?

We often say things we wish we hadn't, or, as we were thinking yesterday, make promises on which we can't or don't follow through.

Not God.

As we have seen, His words and His promises are set in stone and come with the most guaranteed guarantee in the world of guarantees!

His promise today? Never to destroy the whole earth with a flood again. No matter what. He sets a rainbow in the sky (imagine seeing the first ever rainbow, Noah would've been like 'WHAT IS THAT??!!') as a sign and reminder of this promise.

We can rest assured we don't need to fear this kind of judgement from God again. Even more than that, we can rest in the promise we find in Romans 8:1: 'If you belong to Christ Jesus, you won't be punished.' We don't need to fear a flood, but we also don't need to fear what God's judgement will be on us once we leave this world. If we have given our lives to God and asked Him to forgive our sins, then we trust that Jesus has paid for our punishment, and so we are justified before God. That is an amazing truth and one in which we can stand firm, knowing that God is not just a promise-maker, but also a promise-keeper.

GOD FACT: God keeps every single promise He has made. We can be totally confident that He won't change His mind or go back on His word. He will never flood the whole earth again, and He will never condemn anyone who has asked for His forgiveness and trusted in His Son, Jesus Christ.

LIFE HACK: Don't treat God's promises as just inspirational quotes or nice words to stick on your wall. Believe them and use them! Call on God to do as He said! Live today (and the next day, and the next day, and the next day) as someone who truly believes that God has totally and completely dealt with their sin and guilt, and has no punishment waiting ahead!

#ringring

READ GENESIS 12:1-9

Another day, another phone call from a company asking to talk about 'my accident' last year for which I might be due compensation. I was so intrigued by this accident…. When did it happen? What did it involve? Did I suffer memory loss, meaning I have no recollection of ever having been in said accident? The only recent accident I can think of is when I managed to catch both my feet in a plastic bag, fall over and carpet-burn my nose. But I'm pretty sure that was my own fault.

When my phone rings, more often than not it's a nuisance call from some big company trying to make money one way or another. How do I tend to respond to these calls? I don't listen, I politely end the call, hang up and get on with living my life.

However, there are other calls I take very seriously – my manager asking what time I'm due in, my flatmate wondering if I've seen her hairdryer, or my mum asking how I liked the new socks she gave me at Christmas (10/10 gift there, mum!)

In today's passage we see that Abram gets a call. Not from an insurance company, his boss or his mum, but from God. A God he'd never heard from before. But it didn't take him long to suss out that this was the one and only God, the true God. And that this God was an awesome, mighty and holy God who had a right to ask him to uproot his entire life and move away.

Remember, there were no removal vans or new-build apartments. Abram was packing up his belongings, taking his family and going to – well he didn't really know where. But he wasn't about to argue with the maker of the universe. Instead, he made the choice to trust Him.

God might call us to new places too – perhaps not in an audible voice, but in the way He shapes our circumstances. We might face a new home, a new school, or even a new country at different points in our lives. We know far more about God than Abraham did, so how will we respond when He asks us to face new circumstances? Abraham did so with faith and worship. Let's ask God to help us to do the same!

GOD FACT: God often calls His people to new circumstances and challenges. But we can trust Him, even if things are confusing, upsetting, or don't make sense. He had a plan for Abraham, He has a plan for me, and He has a plan for you.

LIFE HACK: Think about something that's changed in your life in the past year. How have you responded to it? It's natural to find change difficult, and God wants us to be honest about where we struggle and what we don't like. But under it all, do we have faith in God's plan? Or do we hold onto a grumbling spirit? Talk to God about it now!

#aintnomountain

READ GENESIS 18:1-15

We skip forward in the story of Abraham today. God has promised Abraham a land that would be filled with his offspring. But Abraham and Sarah had no children and were seriously old at this point. They were thinking less about nappies, and more about zimmer frames!

One day, three mysterious men (AKA God's messengers) arrive at the door and make a CRAY prophecy. Sarah (who is ninety years old) will have had a baby by this time next year. Sarah overhears this incredible claim and what does she do? She has a good giggle! Laughs and laughs and laughs at the idea of someone her age having a little baby.

God's messenger quickly brings a stop to her sniggering by asking, 'Is anything too hard for the Lord?' (verse 14, ESV).

Let me give you a sneak peek at the answer to that one, in case you are unsure.

NO.

Nothing is too hard for God.

Sure enough, by that time the following year, Sarah had given birth to Isaac (which means 'he laughs' – wonder where the inspiration for that name came from, hmmm?!) Isaac grew up to become the father of Jacob, from whom the twelve tribes of Israel descended.

Nothing is too hard for God. Nothing! No person, no situation, no emotion. Nothing.

Now, does this mean we should always expect God to miraculously intervene in our difficult situations? No. Whilst

God can do anything, that doesn't mean He will do anything. His love and wisdom means that He doesn't always give us what we think we want or need.

However, don't let the perceived impossibility of a situation stop you from reaching out to God. Don't be like Sarah and mock the idea of God intervening. Don't limit what God can do by thinking 'this one is just too difficult.' Believe that there is nothing too hard for God.

GOD FACT: Absolutely nothing is too hard for God. Nothing throws Him, confuses Him or is beyond His power to deal with.

LIFE HACK: Think of one situation in your life with which you struggle. Is there a danger of you thinking that God can't help or intervene in it? If so, repent of believing that lie, and ask for God to step in, remembering that nothing and no-one is too hard for God to change.

#goodgifts

READ GENESIS 21:1-7

So, we already know how today's story goes. God keeps His promise to Abraham and Sarah, and little Isaac arrives on the scene, just at the time God said He would.

Perhaps, on reflection, it's easy to think that Abraham and Sarah deserved this little bundle of joy. After all, they had left everything behind to follow God and this was the least He could do for them, right?

Wrong!

When we receive a gift, it's not usually because we've done something. You get presents on your birthday because people love you and want to celebrate your life, you haven't earned them because of your age. (If that was the case, my ninety-one-year-old granny would've gotten a lot more than a mug with my photo on it!)

Likewise, God doesn't give us good gifts because we've earned them through doing 'good' things, or because we deserve them because of how amazing we are. Quite the opposite is true! We owe God everything, and He owes us nothing. The only thing we should expect from Him is His justified wrath but instead, God gives us His generous gifts, day in and day out. It brought Him great joy to give Isaac to Sarah and Abraham, and it gives Him great joy to be generous to you too.

James 1:17 tells us that 'Every good and perfect gift comes down from the Father who created all the lights in the heavens.' That means everything! The shoes on your feet, the joy in your heart, the crisps you ate at lunchtime, the heat in your home, the people in your family and the air that you breathe – all good gifts from Him. Just like Isaac was. You could even argue for the sixteenth series of Spongebob Squarepants you watched on TV!

GOD FACT: He is a generous God who loves to give good gifts to His children!

LIFE HACK: Repent from an entitled heart that thinks it deserves God's kindness. Ask God to give you a grateful heart instead. Right now, think of two things, big or small, that God has given to you today. Then thank Him!

#examtime

READ GENESIS 22:1-19

Yesterday we thought about gifts from God, how we can't claim to either deserve them, or have earned them. There's a hard truth that goes alongside that: God's gifts are God's. That means they aren't ours. Therefore, just as it's His prerogative to give them, it's also His prerogative to take them away.

How did Abraham feel as he trudged towards Moriah with Isaac in tow? He must have been absolutely heartbroken, sick to the stomach, and tormented by the thoughts of what was ahead. His world was spinning with confusion. How could the God in whom he had put his trust, turn out to be so cruel?

Of course, we can only imagine the incredible relief and joy Abraham must have felt when God intervened. God was testing Abraham to see where his heart, his loyalty and his love really lay. Abraham knew that God had forbidden the sacrifice of children (Leviticus 18:21), and so we can imagine that he didn't think Isaac would actually be killed (which Hebrews 11:19 would also suggest). Regardless, this whole scenario must have been incredibly distressing and confusing for Abraham. Even as I read it, I find it hard to truly understand why God put Abraham and Isaac through the wringer in this way!

Perhaps you look at your own life and feel confused, or even distressed. You read about a God who loves and cares for you, but feel that it's difficult to reconcile that with what He's allowing you to go through. Sometimes Christians are tempted to roll out clichés or give pat answers but today's passage demonstrates that our God is a God who sometimes does things we just can't get our head around. And, when that happens, we still need to choose to go God's way. Abraham obeyed God despite not knowing what He was really doing, and sometimes we'll have to do the same.

After his awful experience, Abraham did understand what God had been doing. You will too one day – maybe in this world, maybe in the next. In the meantime, God asks that you trust Him, that you obey Him and that you recognise He is sometimes beyond our understanding.

GOD FACT: God tested Abraham and He will test us with difficult things too. But we can trust that, ultimately, this is going to be for our good, and part of His big Kingdom plan.

LIFE HACK: Think of something in your life in which God doesn't seem very active. Ask Him to change things, and to open your eyes to what He is doing. But also make a decision to willingly submit to His plans, acknowledging that they are above your own.

#thatsmine

READ ALL OF PSALM 24

How often does this phrase cross your mind?

'THAT'S MINE!!' The older you get, the less you might articulate it but the sentiment is often still there!

If any of you have grown up with a sister then you will probably be familiar with this scenario. You come down for breakfast. You pop your cereal in a bowl and stick a piece of bread in the toaster. All is well with the world…until your sister walks in WEARING YOUR CORDUROY DUNGAREES!! How dare she?! They don't belong to her!!

'Take them off!' you exclaim. 'THOSE ARE MINE!'

Even now, when one of my flatmates eats MY chocolate, or my mum uses MY perfume or my friend steals MY joke, I can start to feel mad. Can you sympathise? We all feel we have a right over things that are ours.

If we think about it though, do we really have any right to these things? The short answer is…nope! We don't! Psalm 24 puts it pretty clearly. The earth is the LORD'S and everything in it (which includes my chocolate, dungarees, perfume and hilarious jokes). So before we get super antsy about other people using 'our stuff' we should remember that it's not really 'ours' in the first place. We've been given gifts and God asks us to be generous with how we use them.

Secondly, are you on the earth? Yes? Then you are the Lord's too. You belong to Him. He made you and He has the ultimate say in how you live your life.

He has a right to rule over your life and He has a right to do as He deems best because you belong to Him. But did you really hear that? You are HIS. You are HIS creation. He is so invested in you, because you are part of Him. Don't see yourself as someone being ordered around by a dictator but rather as someone deeply loved by your very own Creator.

GOD FACT: He is a glorious God who has created all things. He deserves so much praise for this and lots of humility in response!

LIFE HACK: Share something today! Be generous towards a friend or family member by sharing something you have, even if it seems small. It was a gift from God, and He is pleased when you don't keep it all to yourself!

#sweetdreams

What sort of a person are you? Do you see the glass as half full or half empty? Are you an optimist or a pessimist? A dreamer or a cynic?

I must confess I tend to fall into the latter camp – if you don't expect too much, you won't be disappointed. Let me give you an example.

It is 14th February – Valentine's Day – and alas, I have failed to find a Valentine. However, a small part of me hopes that perhaps when I return to the flat after work I will find I cannot open the door due to the vast number of cards and gifts which have been sent my way. I get home later that day and unfortunately find the door swings open all too easily.

But wait! There on the floor is a brown envelope addressed to me! I rip it open, read the few short lines and can hardly believe it! I've been asked to keep a certain Tuesday in March free!

For Jury Duty at the High Court.

Not quite the Valentine's date request I had been hoping for. I will now have to wait another year to see if my Valentine's Day dreams are fulfilled!

I recall this story with my tongue planted firmly in my cheek – however, there have been many (far more serious) incidents in my life where I have been very disappointed with how things have turned out. In these situations, it's easy to feel pessimistic and hopeless.

The writer of this Psalm is feeling troubled about the situation he was in. It was most likely written after some of the Israelites in Babylon, who were in exile, were freed from their captivity. But many are still captive, and those who are free are now facing new hardships.

However, instead of dwelling on past disappointments, the psalmist turns his thoughts and prayers to what God had done in the past, and then looks hopefully to the future! The picture he uses is of a farmer going out to sow seed and wetting the ground with his tears. The result is that, after some time, he comes back to reap a big harvest!

Often in life, the hard times that we face are setting us up for something better in the future. The psalmist believes that God will once more step in and bring about a change in His people's fortunes. We too can be expectant that God will show up in our dark seasons, and that He listens when we call on Him to deliver us, as He's done before.

And we can find solace in knowing that, although this world is a place where we will often 'sow in tears', there is a joyful harvest which rests secure, waiting for us to come and enjoy it for eternity.

GOD FACT: God loves to restore. Often He will bless us with a season of joy after a season of hardship. Even if He doesn't, we know we have a harvest beyond imagination coming our way.

LIFE HACK: Pray about something you found disappointing. Recount in prayer what God has done in the past and ask Him to act again!

#icanseeyou

Have you ever found a good hiding place? Like, a really good hiding place? I found one once. We were playing hide and seek at my parents' house and I realised that I could climb into the loft without using the ladder. It was a genius move! Nobody even thought to look up there.

One hour later I finally descended, victorious, awaiting cheers of admiration from my family. Turns out they'd stopped playing ages ago and were now watching Spongebob Squarepants. They'd actually forgotten I was playing…

It's not hard to hide from people, whether that's physically crawling under a bed, or hiding emotionally by not letting anyone know how we really feel.

It might be easy to hide from other people, but it's completely impossible to hide from God. Psalm 139 proves it.

From before you were born (verse 13) God knew you through and through – which means He knows everything about you. Wherever you go in the world (verses 8-9), God will be with you. He is familiar with all your routines (verse 3) and even your sleeping patterns (verse 2 and 18).

There is nothing God doesn't know about you – about your body, your mind, your thoughts, your emotions, your schedule, your relationships, your love of cereal, your favourite karaoke number, and even your dodgy knee that always cracks when you run. He knows it all.

And the best bit is that He doesn't just know, He cares! He's involved! He is crazy about you and is never going to leave you to do life on your own, even if you try to do exactly that (just see verse 10).

Although that's a wonderful truth, it can also be daunting to accept that God knows all. What about the bad parts of me? The jealousy, the lies, the greed, the thoughts and actions that other people would be horrified by? Well, PTL for grace! When God looks at us He sees Jesus' perfection, not the messed up, sinful, selfish creatures that we were before. He has made us new creations! (2 Corinthians 5:17 ESV). Regardless of our behaviour, God promises to be behind, beside and before us, forever.

GOD FACT: God is always with us. It's not dependent on our age, behaviour or geographical location! He is always there, ever-present.

LIFE HACK: Talk to God about a situation that you feel you are dealing with alone. Thank Him for being with you in it and ask Him to help you better discern His love.

#onmyown

READ ALL OF PSALM 88

D o you ever feel lonely? Miserable? Depressed? Do you ever wonder if God is really listening?

All that we read in the Bible is true: God loves us unconditionally and He gives us life in abundance. But being a Christian doesn't magically protect us from the hard parts of life.

When we feel low, it's a good idea to turn to the book of Psalms where the various writers can often be found pouring their hearts out to God. It can help us to know that somebody else has felt the way we do.

The psalmist who wrote Psalm 88 was utterly alone:

'You have taken my companions and loved ones from me; the darkness is my closest friend' (verse 18, NIV).

Sometimes he questioned whether God had abandoned him:

'Why, oh LORD, do you reject me and hide your face from me?' (verse 14, NIV).

He felt overwhelmed with sadness:

'My eyes are dim with grief' (verse 9, NIV).

I love the honesty of this Psalm. The psalmist doesn't give God a short summary of his problems before jumping up with a smile that wouldn't be out of place in a toothpaste advert to give a rousing rendition of 'Father Abraham' (complete with actions). He lets his thoughts and emotions spill out, and articulates in great detail how he really feels.

He knew he could come to God with all his problems and heartbreak, without fearing reprimand.

We can still fully trust God while expressing how we truly feel. He values integrity, and invites us to be honest with Him.

Sometimes as Christians we feel the need to put on a bright smile, give a thumbs up and talk about how much we enjoyed that sermon on Leviticus when, in reality, all we can think about is that crucial exam we've failed or how miserable our home life is.

As encouraging as it is to talk to others about the good things going on in our lives, don't be scared to say, along with the psalmist, that you feel God isn't listening. Remember that, when we do go through 'the valley of darkness', we can be assured that God is with us every step of the way.

'The Lord is close to the broken-hearted and saves those who are crushed in spirit' (Psalm 34:18, NIV).

GOD FACT: God values integrity. He wants us to be honest with each other and with Him about how our life is really going and how we feel. Jesus lived a life here on earth, and suffered more than we can even imagine, so God is under no illusion that life is easy!

LIFE HACK: Talk to God and tell Him how you feel today – even if that feeling is confusion, sadness or anger. He is big enough to take it!

#whatstheplan

Excuses, excuses, excuses. Let's be honest, we do use them from time to time!

My colleague has just asked if I want to come along to the Model Railway show: 'Eh, I'm sorry, but I was planning on watching a documentary about recycling tonight.'

My mum invites me to check out the new compost bins they've stocked in the garden centre: 'Oh I'm sorry, but I've got a sore throat.' (*Cough, cough*).

My friend Jo asks if I'd like to see her new recorder ensemble playing national anthems from around the world: 'Hmm, sounds great, but it's my dog's birthday.'

In today's story, it would've been very tempting for Ruth to make up an excuse to bail on Naomi. Naomi was giving her a clear way out – one that Orpah doesn't need much convincing to take.

But Ruth doesn't go for it. She has made a commitment to this family and is not about to leave, even though there is a very hard path ahead, and she'd already lost so much. It would've been much easier and more comfortable for her to go back to her own family and land. But she doesn't.

She doesn't just think about herself, her own prospects and plans. She thinks about her elderly mother-in-law and decides to stick it out with her. I'm sure Ruth had her own dreams for life which probably did not include a fifty-mile hike with dearest mum-in-law, to a land in which she'd never set foot before; a place where she'd be considered an unwelcome foreigner. But she put her own priorities to one side, and decided to serve someone else.

That must have been very tough! Let's be honest, it's difficult to be more committed to others than to ourselves. Ruth's example is a stellar one!

Despite all this, Ruth was not perfect. I have no doubt she was selfish, and made excuses at other times ('Sorry Naomi, I can't come to your poetry slam tonight. I need to fix my sandals'). She wouldn't have always put others first.

While Ruth might be a great example, the best example of this is Christ. From day one, He has always put His people first. Jesus could have made the choice to stay put in heaven in a perfect home rather than a dirty, messed up, ugly world. But like Ruth, He chose the hard path because His love for you was and is greater than His love for Himself.

GOD FACT: Jesus puts us first. He could have been like Orpah and stayed in home territory, but instead, like Ruth, He gave it all up for others. For us. For you!

LIFE HACK: It's good to dream and make plans about our life. But we need to be willing and ready to set them aside for the sake of others, if that's what God asks us to do. Think of one way in which you could put aside your own plan today to serve someone else.

#whoseplanisitanyway

S o they've arrived...and their stomachs are rumbling! Unfortunately for Ruth and Naomi, there's not exactly a corner shop they can nip into. No twenty-four-hour supermarket ready and waiting. No McDonalds for that Happy Meal they've been dreaming of!

Instead, Ruth volunteers to go and glean in the town fields – picking up what the harvesters have accidentally dropped. This is not glamorous work. It is not work for the well-to-do. It's for the poor and the powerless. For the needy. It must have taken a lot of humility for Ruth to rock up there, knowing that this option was for those at the very bottom of the ladder.

Out of all the fields she could've gone to, Ruth ends up in one that belongs to a relative of Naomi's. A dude called Boaz. WHAT ARE THE CHANCES, HUH?

But of course, there's no Monopoly Chance card at play here. There is only God's plan. As Naomi says in verse 22, Ruth might have been harmed in someone else's field as there was little protection for a foreign woman on her own. God is at work to protect Ruth, to provide for her and Naomi, and to do something so marvellous that, ultimately, it would change world history forever.

More on that tomorrow!

GOD FACT: God has a plan. Nothing is left to chance and nothing happens outside of His control.

LIFE HACK: Pray to God and ask for help to trust Him. Sometimes, we can clearly see what God is up to (it must've been crystal clear to Ruth and Naomi that God was at work here) but at other times, it just makes no sense at all. Ask God to give you peace that He has a big plan, even when things seem to be going wrong.

#actiontime

S o, Ruth has landed herself in Boaz's field. Great. Now what? Naomi believes that God has sent Ruth to Boaz's field as an answer to their prayers. She sees that Ruth could find both a husband and a home in this man, and that he could deliver them both from their difficult situation.

Naomi now sends Ruth out with what seems to us like an odd task.

Nowadays, if you're interested in marrying someone you'd probably go down the flowers, candlelit dinners, 1.5 million-Facebook-pictures-together route – eventually getting down on one knee to pop the big question!

Ruth is doing the Hebrew equivalent. By asking Boaz to spread his garment over her, she is asking him to assume the responsibility for her care, as her husband. It's a symbolic question and act. Now, unfortunately he doesn't respond with a cheesy grin, a big YES, and straight away start booking a harvest-themed engagement photoshoot for the next day. He knows there's somebody ahead of him and that this closer relative would need to have first refusal before he could marry Ruth.

Okay, so this can seem quite weird and confusing to us. But one thing that struck me when reading this passage was that Naomi and Ruth did more than pray, they also acted. They did something!

I have no doubts that they were very prayerful and looked to God for direction, but they didn't just sit back, put their feet up and wait for God to drop a solution into their laps. Naomi came up with a plan, and put it into action!

Sometimes we can face a problem, or see something wrong in the world, and it's natural and good for us to pray about it. Sometimes, however, we stop there when we shouldn't. Struggling at school? Go and speak to your teacher. See someone who is lonely? Befriend them. Saddened by poverty in your community? Get involved with a local charity.

God has given us each a brain in our head and feet in our shoes. Let's not be afraid to use them!

GOD FACT: God always has a plan. But God uses people as part of His plan! He always wants us to be prayerful and wise, but there are times when we need to act and be part of the answer.

LIFE HACK: Think of one thing you've been praying about recently. Ask God to help you think of an action you can take to be part of the change. Then act!

#themasterplan

I t's all kicking off! Boaz wants to marry Ruth and Ruth wants to marry Boaz. Naomi wants Ruth to marry Boaz, too. Sounds great! But then we have another lad thrown into the mix, the kinsman-redeemer! (AKA a male relative who was responsible for the care of a family member in need, and was next in line to receive their land, according to Jewish law.)

Thankfully, it all works out happily ever after. The kinsman-redeemer passes on his chance to marry Ruth, allowing Boaz to sweep her off her feet (which must've been tricky seeing as he only had one sandal on…!).

Like yesterday, the traditions, language and names in this passage can be confusing. Ask God to help you to understand what you find tricky about the passage, but I'd like you to focus on the key word we keep coming across: 'redeem' – which means to buy back. In this story, Boaz was the redeemer. He paid a price, to buy back something that had been lost. Sound familiar?

Jesus was Boaz 2.0. And then some. He paid the ultimate price of taking our punishment on the cross, to redeem us. To buy back something that was lost.

There's a subtle clue that links the two together. Notice who is Obed's grandson? That's right, only King David. Who was, of course, one of the most famous forefathers of Jesus.

In this seemingly insignificant story of a widow and a foreigner, we see mirrored the redemption that Jesus is going to bring, through this very family line. Mind blowing!

Naomi's mates say to her in verses 14-15, 'Praise be to the LORD, who this day has not left you without a kinsman-redeemer… he will renew your life and sustain you' (NIV).

Boaz was a great chap, no doubt about it! He stepped in to save his family (with a bit of prompting!), and Naomi's friends were right to thank God for him. But, as a redeemer, he doesn't even begin to compare to Jesus, who stepped in to save all of mankind.

GOD FACT: God has always had a long term plan for redemption. He has bought back His people and will one day return and restore the world to the way it should be.

LIFE HACK: Thank God for His big plan and praise Him for redeeming you, renewing your life and sustaining you. Naomi and her friends praised God together – share something great God has done in your life with one other person today, as an act of worship.

#thearrival

READ MATTHEW 1:18-25

W e're jumping forward to the birth of the main man Himself – Jesus! But you're probably wondering: mate, why are we reading about the birth of Jesus? It ain't Christmas??

I'll let you in on a little secret that will blow your mind. *whispers* You can read about the birth of Jesus at ANY time of year....wait, whaaat????

So now you've got your head around that, let's look at another (slightly more incredible) truth. Focus in on verse 23. 'A virgin will have a baby boy, and he will be called Immanuel, (which means "God is with us").'

God, who made the entire universe, who is perfectly holy, who is great and mighty, has come down to be with us. US! Tiny, weak, sinful, poor, demanding, annoying, hateful us.

Jesus gave up the perfection of heaven, because He wanted to be with me and to be with you. He gave it all up to live a poor, hard existence so that you could have all the riches of His new Kingdom. He came, as verse 21 tells us, to save His people from their sins, to deliver them from the deathly grip sin holds on mankind.

Don't let that go in one ear and out the other! Think about someone you love – what would you give up for them? Your money? Your health? Your happiness?

What about your life? Maybe, but maybe not. Perhaps that would be just too high a price to pay.

That wasn't the case for Jesus. Jesus gave all that up, and far, far more in order to make a way for you to be redeemed, and for Him to be with you forever! You are that worthwhile and valuable!

GOD FACT: God came to earth in the form of Jesus. He gave up everything in order to become one of us and to save people from their sins, because He loved them and longed to save them from suffering.

LIFE HACK: Listen to the song 'Emmanuel' by Hillsong and reflect on the wonderful truth that God is always with you!

#theteenageyears

READ LUKE 2:41-51

B eing a teenager can be a lot of things. It can be fun, it can be hard, it can be lonely. It can involve dying your hair a colour that was drastically different from what you intended! (To be honest I still do that now and I'm twenty-eight...)

Something that sometimes featured in my teenage years (and maybe yours too) was butting heads with my parents. They seemed to constantly be on my case! Although... I suppose I sometimes did let them down.

I remember one particular occasion when my behaviour disappointed my mother in a rather spectacular fashion. It was a Sunday evening in the height of summer. My family and I had been visiting relatives, and we were now making our way out of church. While my brothers and I ran ahead, my mum walked more slowly with a friend who had a young family of her own. Having seen her small children sit so quietly in church, my mum commented on how lovely and well-behaved they were. Her friend responded with thanks, and added that she was very impressed that my siblings and I got on so well, and acted with such maturity.

Just as she finished speaking, both she and my mother walked around the corner to find me banging my younger brother's head off the car bonnet, in an attempt to prevent him from sitting in the front seat of the car... My mum was understandably disappointed in my behaviour, and I had to sit in the back seat the whole way home.

So how is it that Jesus gets off the hook? He's caused a bit of a mare here by disappearing off back to the temple! Eventually, when His parents find Him, he appears to get away with it by mentioning something about being in His Father's house!

However, what Jesus was saying was seriously profound. He was reminding His earthly parents (and us), that there was a higher authority that He answered to, and that He was on earth to carry out God's plans and not theirs. They don't really get it, but Mary does 'treasure these things' in her heart – while she might not understand them, she doesn't dismiss them.

So what about you and me? Does that mean we can wander off to church instead of going to visit Great Aunt Elspeth with our dad? No, it doesn't. Jesus was one of a kind. His calling was to do His Father's will in saving mankind. That's not our calling. God's will for us is that we obey our parents, just as Jesus obeyed His. He knows that's not easy, especially when they act in ways that we don't respect – but God is the one who has decided who our parents will be, and He asks us to honour them for that reason.

GOD FACT: Jesus was the Son of God and God was the ultimate authority in His life. He knew what He was on earth to do, and He did it perfectly. God chooses who your parents will be, and asks you to respect and honour His choice.

LIFE HACK: Next time a situation turns up where you are struggling to obey your parents, pray to God (right then and there!) and ask Him for His help to obey His command to honour them.

#thecousin

READ LUKE 3:1-22

W e've all got that slightly odd family member, haven't we? The one who has a pet llama called Robert, or is a professional tiddlywinks player, or wears shorts all year round! There's one in every family.

Jesus had a kinda weird family member: His cousin John. John did slightly bizarre things. He lived in the desert, wore camel clothes and ate locusts for fun. He was quite shouty and probably had a serious beard going on.

However, John wasn't some crazy lad who had a great love of wild camping and ethically sourced fashion He had a God appointed role, and he was giving it his all! His job was to get people ready for Jesus coming. He was to warn them that they were in serious trouble because of their sin and that he was someone they needed to listen to. A voice of love and salvation!

'A voice of one calling in the desert, "Prepare the way for the Lord."'

Jesus comes to visit one day, and John baptises Him (verse 21). That must've been an incredibly special moment for them both! It's made even more incredible by God's voice coming from heaven, bursting with pride. 'You are my own dear Son, and I am pleased with you.'

This must've been a knock-out day for John. Maybe he could have splashed out and had a proper meal in celebration. Who knows?

What we do know is that we can join in that celebration (although let's stick to eating crisps yeah?). Although John was privileged to be Jesus' cousin, the brilliant truth is that we are made Christ's brothers and sisters – through His death.

When people look at you, they might think you are great, they might think you are weird, they might think you are unimportant. Celebrate today because God looks at you and says 'You are my own dear child, and I am pleased with you.' Hallelujah!

GOD FACT: God was, and is, fully pleased with Jesus, and with you!

LIFE HACK: Give thanks to God and do something to celebrate being part of God's family as a loved child! Sing a song, do a little dance, eat some of your favourite food and bask in God's goodness! And, the next time you see that slightly odd family member of yours, tell them they are loved (and that their mime artistry is epic!).

#thedesert

READ LUKE 4:1-15

S o Jesus has just been baptised, heard God's voice from heaven, and had the Holy Spirit descend on Him… So, what's next? Perhaps you'd expect Him to go out and start His ministry with a bang! Instead, the Spirit leads Him into the desert. Seems odd? Who exactly is He going to share His message with out there? A camel??

Jesus is preparing to begin His ministry and He uses this time to fast and pray so He will be spiritually prepared for the battle ahead. Now, I don't know about you, but I usually start to feel a bit faint if I don't get my breakfast, never mind fasting for forty days! Jesus must've been extremely weak, tired and hungry – and that's exactly when the devil strikes!

The devil hopes he can stop Jesus before He even begins His work and cleverly tries to use the Bible – God's own words – to trip Jesus up. It was a battle for sure, but at every attempt, Jesus has a rebuttal! He trumps the devil's lies with God's truth.

Imagine it. Forty days without food and without any friends to help you through. Knowing that what lies ahead is a hard, hard job which will lead to an unimaginably torturous death (both physically and spiritually). The devil is relentlessly tempting Jesus. He's really trying his hardest, using the Father's own words, to get Jesus to give in. Don't be fooled into thinking that because Jesus was God, this was easy for Him. He was both fully God AND fully man, and would've struggled in exactly the same way we do.

Despite the struggle, He didn't give in. What's the end result? The clue is in verse 14 – He returned to Galilee in 'the power of the Spirit.' He must've been physically exhausted but He was spiritually strong and ready to head out on a mission that would change the world forever.

Hebrews 2:18: 'And now that Jesus has suffered and was tempted, He can help anyone else who is tempted.'

GOD FACT: Jesus was tempted just like we are. It was incredibly hard for Him not to give in to that temptation. As the writer of Hebrews tells us, He knows the suffering of temptation. He knows how hard and miserable it is, but because of that, He can help us!

LIFE HACK: Think of an area of temptation that you are struggling with. Remind Jesus what it's like to be in that place, then ask Him to help you. Meditate on the truth that we receive a spiritual power boost when we say no to the wrong path.

#whoyouare

We step forward in time to today's passage, where Jesus has called His disciples and begun His ministry. They're journeying back to Galilee and have to go through a Samarian town. The Samaritans and the Jews were enemies and, as such, the disciples wouldn't have been particularly psyched about travelling through this particular neck of the woods. Once they arrive, the disciples head off to get some food, and an exhausted Jesus takes a seat by the local well.

Along comes a Samaritan woman, who nearly keels over when Jesus asks her for a drink. He's a Jew, and a man…why would He stop to chat with her?!

And so a very interesting dialogue begins. The conversation seems to revolve around water and thirst, but it takes our Samaritan pal a while to clock that Jesus is talking about the Spirit rather than actual H_2O! She is completely taken aback when Jesus reveals His knowledge of her 'interesting' life choices. She tries to deflect by talking about the difference in religious viewpoints between the Jews and Samaritans, but eventually gets down to the nitty gritty by expressing her hope for the coming Messiah. And Jesus lets her in on a little known fact – that's Him!

There's lots and lots packed into this passage, but let's focus on that last answer from Jesus in verse 26 (NIV): 'I who speak to you am He.'

To this small, sinful, 'enemy' woman Jesus clearly reveals Himself as Messiah. Besides His disciples, we have no record of Jesus being this clear with anyone else about who He is. But wait, why? Why didn't He print the announcement in the 'Daily Scroll', or speak to kings and rulers?

I think Jesus did this to show the kind of person He had come to earth for. Of course, the Kingdom doors are open to everyone, but here, Jesus is demonstrating that those who the world would label a 'nobody' are absolutely a 'somebody' in His eyes.

At the time, Jesus only explicitly shared His identity with this one woman, but the record of the conversation in John's gospel means that Jesus is now telling millions of people (including you!) that, 'I am He'.

How did the Samaritan woman respond? See verse 29 – with belief, joy and by sharing the good news. What is your response to being let in on Jesus' true identity?

GOD FACT: Jesus was the Messiah, and He was clearest about this fact to a 'nobody'.

LIFE HACK: Give thanks to God that He has been so clear with you about who He is. Ask Him for the opportunity to share that knowledge today with someone whom the world doesn't value.

#nocrustsplease

I was attending a conference and it had been a bit of a long day. The seminars were over, and now it was dinner time. Sitting around the table with a number of people I didn't know, I tried to make conversation with the girl to my right. We covered where we were from, our jobs, hobbies, family, and then it started to get a bit quiet. In a desperate attempt to keep the conversation going, I hit out with this rather pathetic question:

'So, what's your favourite kind of bread?'

Hmmm…don't think I'll be writing a book on the art of conversation any time soon!

The strange thing was that everyone around the table eventually started talking about their favourite kind of bread! Because almost everybody does eat some kind of bread; in most countries and cultures throughout the world, bread is a feature!

So when Jesus says He is 'The Bread of Life', what is He on about? A sandwich option we didn't know about? A spiritual meal deal? Unsurprisingly, it's a bit more complex than that.

Jesus brings up the whole bread issue because the crowd following Him have just experienced (or heard about) Him miraculously feeding a crowd of people. They want more! Just not more of Jesus. More of the show-stopping miracles, and the free wheaty goodness he miraculously provides instead!

Jesus calls them out on it. He uses their bread obsession to tell them more about who He really is. 'I am the bread that gives life! No one who comes to me will ever be hungry' (verse 35). A bit like what He said to the woman at the well, Jesus tells the crowd that He can give them a spiritual wholeness that will satisfy them forever. Jesus is to the soul what bread is to our stomachs! Satisfying, nourishing and life-giving (unless you're gluten intolerant, but hopefully you can still get the picture!).

The crowd don't really get it. They bang on about God providing for Moses and the Israelites in the Old Testament without clocking that an infinitely more amazing provision is standing right before their eyes! They think that because they know Jesus' earthly parents (who were normal, run-of-the-mill types) that Jesus can't be anything special either. They have the option of eternal life-giving bread, but they'd rather a peanut and jelly sandwich and a show.

Verse 27 warns us, 'Don't work for food that spoils. Work for food that gives eternal life'.

The crowd didn't heed it. Let's not make the same mistake!

GOD FACT: God sent Jesus, the Bread of Life. Jesus referred to Himself in this way to show that what He offered was satisfying, nourishing and life-giving.

LIFE HACK: You don't have one almighty baguette on a Sunday and expect it to see you through to next week; likewise we need to be coming to the Bread of Life daily! If you want more than 'stuff and a show' from Jesus, then you need to spend time in His Word and chatting with Him every day. That way you'll be fed and built up! Why not have a spiritual snack right now?

#lightoflife

READ JOHN 8:12-20

We've all been there. It's the middle of the night and you really need a glass of water – but you don't want to wake up your mum or the monsters under your bed, so you try and get to the kitchen without putting any lights on. You stagger through, arms outstretched to try and prevent the almost inevitable toe stubbing. You fumble about to find the door handle, eventually swinging the kitchen door open, before accidentally standing on the cat (who already doesn't like you). The cat makes a noise like…well, an angry cat, and you wonder if turning the hall light on was maybe the quicker and quieter way to fulfil your watery quest!

We need light to live. Try writing, cooking or playing lacrosse in the dark and see how you fare! Life is difficult and dangerous in the darkness.

When Jesus claims to be 'the light of the world' (verse 12), He is talking about much more than avoiding accidentally kicking your cat in the dark. When He spoke these words, He was standing in the part of the temple that held the four giant candelabra. When they were lit, they flung light across the city which, considering there were no street lamps, bedside lamps, or lava lamps, would've been very impressive! They were lit to remind the Jewish people of how God had used the pillar of fire to lead His people through the desert, in the time of Moses.

So when Jesus says He is the light of the world, He is calling His listeners to think not just about the huge lights right in front of them, but also the pillar of fire; and how He is like them both.

Light lets you see what's really going on. Light takes away fear and brings you joy. Light enables you to get on with everyday living. Light sustains our planet and, in fact, our very lives. The light of the pillar of fire protected and led those who followed it… Jesus is telling the crowd then, and us now, that He doesn't just provide physical light for us but, more importantly, that He is spiritual light in our dark world.

'Whoever follows me will never walk in darkness' (verse 12 NIV).

As the cat discovered, darkness is confusing and dangerous. Without Jesus (the light of life), life is dark and dead – you can't see where you are going, what's happening around you, or receive true life. The Pharisees chose this darkness. They refused to believe Jesus and, because of their choice, couldn't see who Jesus, or His Father, truly were.

The choice is ours: darkness or the light of life.

Matthew 4:16: 'Although your people live in darkness they will see a bright light. Although they live in the shadow of death a light will shine on them.'

GOD FACT: Jesus is the light of the world, and we never have to be without the presence of the light of life.

LIFE HACK: Jesus openly spoke about who He was, because He didn't want people to live in a dark world. Pray for Jesus to shine a light into a part of your neighbourhood or school where you perceive there to be real spiritual darkness.

#whatsnewwithewe

READ JOHN 10:1-21

L et's be honest, there are a lot of sheep in the Bible. They seem to get everywhere. Particularly in John 10! Sheep all over the shop!

There's LOTS of sheep-related imagery in this passage, and it can be confusing to understand what all these different pictures about our woolly friends mean! So let's focus on one particular message.

Jesus says: 'I tell you the truth, I am the gate for the sheep. Whoever enters through me will be saved' (verse 9, NIV).

I'm going to take a guess that we all know how a gate functions and what it looks like. If you're a sheep (which I doubt any of you readers are), you'd have a hard time getting into the field over the wall. You're not going to have much luck with a ladder either. Or a parachute drop. Tunnelling underground isn't really an option. The gate is the only way you are getting into that field. The only way you're getting home.

Jesus is telling us that He is the only way for us to be made right with God, to 'enter' into our true home. We can't be good enough, or clever enough, or woolly enough! Through Him is the only way.

When we do enter, we find grass (sustenance), and wolf proof walls (security)! Jesus (the gate) is between us and our enemy (the devil), so we don't need to fear once we're safely inside.

'I have come that they may have life, and have it to the full' (verse 10, NIV).

Life as a Christian doesn't always feel that way though. It can seem restrictive and even (dare I say it) boring! But when Jesus talks about life, He doesn't mean having the best-time-ever-all-the-time-can't-stop-smiling type life, He is talking about never-ending, soul-reviving, heart-restoring, grace-filled, God-infused LIFE! A life that no-one can ever take away from you. A place in your true home for which you'll never have to pay rent, or worry about getting chucked out. An eternity that is more awesome, fun and colourful than you could ever possibly imagine.

GOD FACT: Sin has caused a barrier between us and God. Jesus is the gate – a way through that barrier!

LIFE HACK: Thank Jesus that He has given us a way to enter into true life. Spend a bit of time imagining the things about the new world that you'll enjoy the most, even if it's a small thing! (I like thinking about how I'll have the time and opportunity to go on travels and adventures that I'll never have time for in this world!)

#feelingsheepish

READ ALL OF JOHN 10:1-21 (AGAIN!)

We're back in John 10 today because, as I'm sure we can agree, it's not a baaa-d idea to read it again! Please don't lamb-ent the fact that these puns are so bad, they are all I've goat, but I'll try not to ram them down your throat…!

Several times in John 10, Jesus refers to Himself as 'the good shepherd'.

What does a shepherd do? He (or she) looks after the sheep of course! In Jesus' day and location, there was a real threat from wild animals, so this was not a particularly easy or safe job. Jesus speaks of how the Good Shepherd doesn't run away from this danger. In fact, His flock are so important to Him, He'd rather die defending them than let the wolves rip them to pieces.

Sound familiar?

If you doubt God's love for you, just take a minute to meditate on that image. The Good Shepherd would rather die than let His sheep be destroyed. Jesus preferred to die rather than give you over to misery and death. Even though you're just a plain old sheep. To Him, your value is beyond measure.

One other thing – if you have a pet, you'll know that it recognises your voice. If I came and yelled 'WALKIES' at your cat, it probably wouldn't respond! Likewise, sheep recognise the voice of the Shepherd and know it's safe to follow.

If you're part of this flock, then be encouraged that you do know Jesus' voice, and that you can recognise what He is saying. It says so, right here! Sheep might be limited in their understanding (a shepherd telling his flock about his tax return is not going to get much of a response!), but they can hear and recognise the shepherd's voice – so be encouraged that the same is true for you! Whether it's a small internal voice, advice from a friend, a change in circumstances, a sermon you hear, a dream, or through reading the Bible, you can hear!

GOD FACT: Jesus chose to protect His flock by laying down His life. He also speaks, and can be heard by His sheep.

LIFE HACK: Think of something you need help or guidance with and ask Jesus to speak to you about it. Put a timer on your phone for three minutes, and just listen. Jesus will guide you and you will recognise His leading.

#lifeparttwo

READ JOHN 11:1-44

It was a quiet Friday afternoon and, in the sleepy atmosphere of the office, time was crawling by. I was considering a trip to the bakers to purchase a snack (19p chocolate-sprinkled pastry, hello!) when suddenly the fire alarm began to screech!

As all good British people would, I looked over to my manager to see what she would do, instead of getting myself out of the building as fast as humanly possible. She sat for a moment before grabbing her jacket and heading for the door, prompting me to do the same.

We got down to the car park where the caretaker was waiting for us. It turned out it was just a drill and I did not need to fear the fate of my secret chocolate stash, hidden in my desk drawer.

After being informed that there was no fire, we turned to head back into the building. But the caretaker stopped us. The drill was not finished. Before we were allowed back in, he needed my manager to carry out a roll call to account for all workers. It went something like this:

Manager: 'ML'

Me: 'Here'.

With the world's longest roll call completed, the three of us trooped back inside.

Today's reading also features a very small roll call, with just the one name – Lazarus. But the outcome of his tale is a tad more exciting!

Jesus restores Lazarus to life, which was an amazing miracle. But the Bible tells us that Lazarus isn't the only one whose name Jesus will call back from death. As Martha says, she knows that Lazarus will rise again in the resurrection at the last day. Jesus then declares Himself to be 'the resurrection and the life' meaning that He IS the source of life and victory over the grave.

1 Thessalonians 4:16: 'With a loud command and with the shout of the chief angel and a blast of God's trumpet, the Lord will return from heaven. Then those who had faith in Christ before they died will be raised to life.'

When Jesus returns, He will call Lazarus' name, but if you have put your trust in Him – the resurrection and the life – then He will also call yours. Lazarus 2.0!

I am very glad that my name is on the fire drill roll call at work and I'm working to get 'ML's secret chocolate stash' also added to the list! However, there is an infinitely more important roll call that I know my name is on and that's the only one that really matters.

We'll be coming back to this story again, keep your eyes peeled! (Whatever that means? It sounds gross! Just to be clear, please don't actually peel your eyes – just keep this story in mind!).

GOD FACT: He is LIFE and He has overcome death. When Jesus returns He'll call our name and we'll join Him, fully restored to life as it should be. He'll call out the names of His children, those who trust in His salvation, and they'll join Him.

LIFE HACK: Do you trust in God? Yes? Then thank God that just like Lazarus, He will call your name and defeat death forever! If something is getting you down today, remember that the day will come when it will all be forgotten, just as Mary and Martha's grief was.

#threeforthepriceofone

READ JOHN 14:1-14

How do I get to work in the morning? Well, there are three main options.

1)   On the pavement along the main road.

– Pros: mostly downhill.

– Cons: lots of other people, inevitably walking more slowly than I am and leaving little space for a sneaky overtake.

2)   Down the path between the flats.

– Pros: fewer people.

– Cons: the neighbour's dog, Duncan (Who names their dog Duncan?) also likes going this way and I am afraid of him. He is small but mean.

3)   Up the back road by the shops.

– Pros: I can stop at the shops for a pre-work Freddo (frog made of chocolate in case you don't know. No, not an actual frog – just a pretend one!).

– Cons: I arrive at work feeling a bit sick after eating said Freddo while jogging. (Jogging because I have made myself late by stopping to buy the Freddo.)

Other alternatives include: hiring a camel, using a pogo stick, or forming a huge conga line. There are so many options that I've had to try and work out which one is best. (I've gone for Option 1. Slow but safe.)

When it comes to finding a way to God, it might seem like there are endless possibilities, but Jesus makes it clear that there's just one. Him. He is the way. Well...that made things easy!

Unlike my selection of journeys, there aren't any 'cons' when it comes to Him. In fact, there are just more and more 'pros'! He is the way to God, the eternal truth and the source of life!

It can sometimes feel like God is far away. Or that He's far too busy with big picture stuff to care about a small, insignificant human who's scared of a dog named Duncan! But Jesus tells us that He is the only way for us to be friends with the God of the universe. And that this was a way God was desperate to create! He wouldn't have gone to such lengths if He wasn't truly interested in having a relationship with us.

GOD FACT: It's not difficult, or complex to know God – because He sent Jesus. God loved us so deeply He went to epic lengths to create a way for us to be restored, and to know Him.

LIFE HACK: Think of something that you feel is too insignificant for God to care about or intervene in. Thank Jesus for opening up a way to God, and tell Him about your problem. Ask Him to act, trusting that He cares about you.

#grapeplant

READ JOHN 15:1-8

I t's our last 'I am' saying and – good news – it's about fruit so you can totally count reading this as one of your five a day.

We don't know what inspired Jesus to give this picture. Perhaps He saw a vineyard in the distance, or maybe one of the disciples bought a nice Pinot Grigio to have with dinner. Regardless, Jesus wants His disciples to think about how the grapes are produced. He explains how the vine sustains the branches, providing them with the required nutrients to grow fruit. Do you see the similarities?

We can only bear fruit (become more like Christ) if we're connected to and rooted in Him. If we're just trying on our own, we'll ultimately fail because 'no branch can bear fruit by itself'.

It's God who grows us! But what's required of us? To remain in Him. That means that we should be fully committed to Him – listening to Him, following Him, feeding from Him through His Word.

Watch out for the warning here in verse 2:

'He cuts away every branch of mine that doesn't produce fruit. But He trims clean every branch that does produce fruit, so that it will produce even more fruit.' Ouch.

A branch that does not bear fruit is getting the chop! What does Jesus mean? Well, He's talking about someone who has stopped (or never started) receiving growing goodness from God. Someone who believes they can do it all alone. They've rejected God, so He cuts them away from His family. If you're worried that might be you, chill out! A concern about bearing fruit is a sign that you do care, and that you are looking to Jesus to grow.

But He also says He trims the branches that are doing well. What?! That sounds painful!

Yes, it is! When God grows us, it isn't easy or pain free. Often it's the opposite. Despite this, we can be encouraged that this 'pruning' is both for our good and for the good of His Kingdom. Ultimately, it brings about more growth, and more harvest.

Theodore Roosevelt said (quite a long time ago, but still relevant today):

'Nothing in the world is worth having or worth doing unless it means effort, pain, difficulty.'

I think that's true! If we want to see worthwhile fruit, then we can't expect it to be a breeze. There will be pruning, and plenty of it. But we can rest assured that the gardener is connected to the vine, who is connected to the branches, and He's never going to clip something that won't grow back bigger and better!

GOD FACT: God grows us and uses us to bear fruit, if we remain in Him.

LIFE HACK: Read James 1:1-5 and pray that God would help you to see the value of 'pruning'. Even though it seems impossible, ask that you would be able to consider joyfully the hard things He is using in your life to grow you!

#mountainshoutin

READ MATTHEW 5:1-12

So now we know a bit about who Jesus says He is, and what that tells us about God's character and plan. But what did Jesus have to say to the people around Him? The people who saw Him every day? Well, quite a bit it turns out!

In the now famous 'Sermon on the Mount', Jesus told the crowds all about what His Kingdom looked like – and it would have been totally shocking to those who heard it. The belief of the day was that the rich and prosperous were the ones who were a sure thing for God's Kingdom. They also believed that it was fair to give someone exactly what they deserved ('an eye for an eye').

The phrase 'poor in spirit' can be a confusing one. Is it talking about a ghost that's hit hard times? Not quite. It describes a recognition that you have nothing to offer God, a realisation that spiritually speaking, you are impoverished. Likewise, 'those who mourn' describe people who recognise the sin within them and are saddened by it. Thankfully, instead of getting angry at people who realise they aren't up to scratch, Jesus says something extraordinary. They are the ones who are blessed and they are the ones who will receive what they know they don't deserve – a spot in His Kingdom.

He continues to give a rundown of His Kingdom comrades and, in the eyes of the world, they are the most unlikely candidates! Being meek (humble, quietly enduring difficult people and situations) is not exactly something most people would stick on a CV! Often those who are merciful are viewed as weak. But God tells us it's these kinds of people who will inherit His Kingdom. They are the people He will bless (show special favour to). Jesus presents this topsy-turvy Kingdom, and it blows the people's minds! What reaction does it bring about in you?

GOD FACT: Jesus told the crowd (and now tells us) that His Kingdom doesn't prioritise the glamorous, the rich, the powerful, or the strong when it comes to recruitment (although they are more than welcome). Instead He is the God of the meek, the humble, the merciful, the peace-makers, the picked-on, the righteousness-seekers, the pure-hearted, the sin-mourners. Those who can see and admit that they are messed up, ugly sinners who have thought and done things they'd never want to tell another living soul about. Those who realise there is no way they are 'good enough'. THOSE people are welcomed to the Kingdom, and blessed!

LIFE HACK: If you know you are a messed up, ugly sinner then thank God that He has dealt with all that, and made you a new creation. Thank Him for opening up the way for you to be blessed, and to be part of His Kingdom. Look for an opportunity today to be a peace-maker, even if it's just in a small way.

#itsnotaboutthemoney

As we learned yesterday, the Jews of Jesus' time believed that wealthy people were rich because God liked them so much, so the disciples are stunned by this interaction with Jesus and Mega-Bucks McGee! They assumed the man's great wealth meant he was a shoo-in for God's Kingdom, but Jesus revealed the young lad loved his money far more than he loved God.

So what does this story mean? That we should sell our Converse, Samsung Galaxy and stuffed Pikachu toy in order to make it to heaven? No, that's definitely not the message Matthew wants us to take away.

This young man was confident in his own goodness. He claims to have followed ALL the commands since we was just a tot, but, as we saw yesterday, that's not going to hack it when it comes to God's Kingdom. Of course, Jesus knows the state of this chap's heart, and knew that money was the real 'god' he worshipped. He challenged him to remove that 'god' (see verse 21). What was his reaction? The young man went away sad, because he loved his money too much to want to part with it.

So what about us? Does God want us to give up things we enjoy because He's some sort of weird buzz-kill? Does Jesus not like us to be happy? Does he not want to compete with X-box and Adidas trainers?

Not at all! The Bible tells us that God gives us all the good things in this world for gifts, and He loves to see us enjoy them. He makes it clear that there's nothing wrong with being rich (in fact there are many people in the Bible whom God blesses with wealth, like Abraham and Solomon) and so we shouldn't feel guilty about enjoying the things He has blessed us with.

The problem starts when our love for something grows bigger than our love for God. When our dedication to something is bigger that our dedication to God, and when our number one heart's desire is actually for wealth (or Converse, Samsung Galaxy, stuffed Pikachu, etc.) and not Him. It's not right and it's not good. It's sin. Any 'god' we have instead of Jesus will inevitably be destructive to us.

Jesus didn't call this guy out because He wanted to shame him, or send him off crying, hoping that, one day, the young man would see that money would never be enough, but that God would always be enough. He did it because He loved Him and He could see that money was ruining him. He wanted to free him from its grip. The man went away sad, but I have no doubt that Jesus went away sadder, knowing that this man had chosen money rather than true riches. One day, the young man would see that money would never be enough, but that God would always be enough.

GOD FACT: God wants our hearts! Not because He hates competition or is greedy, but because He loves us and knows that any other idol we set up in our life will cause misery and destruction.

LIFE HACK: Think of something you are tempted to 'worship', to make more important than Jesus in your life (e.g. happiness, popularity, clothes, the opposite sex, money, music). Ask God for help to stop it becoming 'King' in His place.

#workingninetofive

READ MATTHEW 20:1-16

L ife's not fair! Have you ever felt that way? Life was
very unfair to me recently when a friend who's a flight
attendant brought me on a trip to Jamaica. For free.

That's right. FREE.

Didn't pay for the flight, the hotel, the food, the rental
tandem…nada! Perhaps other guests at the resort would've
been annoyed to know that while they'd paid full price, I was
paying nothing. (TBH, I already looked out of place. While they
rummaged for sun cream from designer handbags, I tried to
quickly whip mine out from my Tesco Bag For Life). They had
paid hundreds, if not thousands of pounds to be there…so
why had I got to go for free? It wasn't fair! But because of my
generous friend and her generous employer, I was benefitting
from that unfairness.

When I read this parable, it seems CRAY unfair. Why should
the lazy sods at the end get just as much as the hardworking
souls from the start?

Just to be clear, Jesus' parable is not about paying wages.
His parable is about grace! Which God's Kingdom is all about!
Forgiveness means that you don't get what you deserve (which
is pretty brilliant), but grace is about getting far more than you
deserve (which is nothing short of epic)!

This parable shows that God's grace isn't earned by hard
work and a good CV. Nobody deserves grace and that's why God
pours it out equally to the top-missionary-amazing-Christian
and the barely-getting-by-watches-Netflix-all-day-Christian. Both
are just as undeserving and neither can do anything more, or
anything less to 'earn' God's grace. Hooray!

A bit like my free holiday, God's grace is unfair, but you and I depend on that 'unfairness' because we don't deserve it any more than the 'lowest of the low' of this world.

'For by grace you have been saved through faith. And this is not your own doing; it is the gift of God, not a result of works, so that no one may boast.' (Ephesians 2:8-9 ESV).

GOD FACT: God's Kingdom is all about grace, which He gives to all His children in equal measure. 'Hard work' doesn't equate to more grace because it can't be earned!

LIFE HACK: Ask God to give you a better handle on grace. Can you think of anyone God has blessed in a way that has made you respond with 'that's not fair!'? Then ask for forgiveness, and for Him to change your heart so that you can simply be happy for them!

#rumblingtummies

C an you imagine the scene? Five thousand men, joined by a good number of women and children, all looking about for something to sink their teeth into! But with no McDonalds or KFC nearby, it was turning into an issue.

Well, not for Jesus it wasn't. He knew God would provide, and with the little that the young lad offered (kudos to him for sacrificing his packed lunch), the crowds were miraculously fed and there were even basketfuls left over! (People obviously didn't like their crusts 2,000 years ago either…)

It must have been incredible.

Once again, the crowds continue to follow Jesus, eager to…. have another panini. Jesus spots their motivation right away! 'You are looking for me, not because you saw miraculous signs but because you ate the loaves and had your fill' (John 6:26 NIV).

Jesus could perceive that the crowds following Him were mostly people who weren't genuinely interested in Him and His Kingdom. They didn't want to find out how the miraculous signs told them about who He truly was, and what He was about. All they really wanted was full bellies.

What about you? I know that there are times I just want God for the 'benefits' and not because I am wholeheartedly committed to following Him. I want His help and friendship, the material blessings and the nice church to attend – but am I loving Him for who He is, or for the good things He gives me? Am I still 'all in' when these good things are less apparent in my life?

It's great when God gives bread, waffles, burgers, friends, good school grades, help in trouble, recovered health, (reruns of Spongebob Sqaurepants?) and answered prayer! But if all we are

interested in is the 'stuff' then we'll end up like these crowds –
physically fed but spiritually starving.

GOD FACT: God is provider of all things and He loves to give
us good things!

LIFE HACK: Trust God to provide what you need today, and
ask Him to help you love Him for who He is and not just the good
stuff that He brings.

#waterwalker

READ JOHN 6:16-24

What do you find scary? Spiders? Heights? The prospect of your Great Aunt Edna giving you one of her sloppy kisses?

I don't really blame the disciples for freaking out when they see Jesus walking on the water – just try to imagine what that would've looked like! One minute you're straining at the oars, the next thing you're seeing a strange figure casually strolling towards you across the waves. Personally, I think I would have grabbed my armbands and headed for the shore!

When Jesus gets close enough, He says to them, 'It is I; don't be afraid' (verse 20, NIV) and this immediately quells their fears. They know who He is. They know He's not a ghost, a scary merman, or a very weirdly shaped fish. They recognise that it's their friend Jesus, and they let Him hop in the boat.

I'm sure they were still totally thrown by it all. How was Jesus able to walk on water? Why was Jesus walking on water? Why hadn't He warned them about what He was going to do? But they didn't need to know the answers to those questions before they let Him in, they just needed to know Jesus was there and they didn't need to be afraid.

We all face circumstances where we don't get what's going on. I doubt anyone is facing any water-walking issues, but there are lots of times in life we have questions about what God is doing and why. His way can seem strange, and scary.

Much like the disciples, we may or may not get the answers to our questions but what we'll definitely get is Jesus Himself, telling us, 'It's me; don't be scared.' Whatever path we are facing we can know God has a plan, Jesus is with us, and that we don't need to be afraid.

GOD FACT: God is totally trustworthy, but He is also a God who works in mysterious ways – ways that we can't always figure out. 'How great is God—beyond our understanding!' (Job 36:26 NIV).

LIFE HACK: The disciples knew and trusted Jesus. In the confusing storms of our life, we can do the same. His presence means we don't need to be afraid, even when His actions can be confusing. If you're facing a confusing storm at the moment, ask Jesus to remind you who He is and to give you peace.

#Lazarusraised

READ JOHN 11:1-44 (YES, WE'VE ALREADY READ IT –
WE'RE GOING TO READ IT AGAIN! ROUND 2!)

Are you a crier? I'm usually not, but occasionally there are exceptions. Last Christmas, for example, when I first saw the 'Holidays Are Coming' advert from Coca-Cola (which in my mind marks the start of the Christmas season), I was so excited I started blubbering.

More seriously, I've had a number of things I've shed tears about over the last year that have not been due to how happy I was. My granny passed away, a good friend was diagnosed with a serious illness, my job was extremely stressful, I missed a friend who had moved away...the list goes on.

The story of Lazarus is MIND BLOWING. We've already thought about Jesus' claim to be 'the resurrection and the life', but this time I want to focus on a different element of the story. The crying.

John 11:35: 'Jesus wept'. (Shortest verse in the Bible in case that ever comes up in a quiz!)

Jesus saw that His friend was dead and even though He knew he would be resurrected, He just stood there and cried. He didn't tell everyone to cheer up, He didn't scold them and say they should always be joyful. He didn't read them a Bible verse, sing 'He's got the whole world', or tell them, 'Hey guys, all things work together for good!' He just cried with His heartbroken friends.

When things are bad in life (and, spoiler alert, they often will be!) we can be tempted to feel like God wants us to put on a brave face, to look for the silver lining, or to tell everyone that we are filled with peace/joy/fibre.

In actual fact, Jesus shows us here that it's ok just to be sad about a thing. It's ok to admit that something is rubbish. It's ok to experience grief without sugar-coating the experience.

Jesus saw that death was awful and He wept about it with His friends. Period.

Of course, He went on to raise Lazarus, and even greater than that, His ministry ended in His total defeat of death on the cross! Lazarus' story ended in joy, and so will ours, hallelujah!! But in the meantime, we don't need to always wear a smile and give an incessant thumbs up. Jesus wept, and we should too.

GOD FACT: In hard times, God is not one who stands aloof, awkwardly pats us on the shoulder or tells us, 'buck up, you've lots to be thankful for'. He is a friend who weeps alongside us.

LIFE HACK: Be honest with God about how things are. Forget trying to impress Him, or show Him your wonderfully positive attitude! He values integrity and knows the ups and downs of living in this world first-hand.

#thelittledudes

READ LUKE 10:21 AND 18:15-17

L et's be honest, little kids can be annoying. And they can be harsh. I sometimes work with young children in my job, and it can be really trying. Just the other day I was in a classroom with some five-year-olds. I sat on the floor, and said to them, 'It's great to see you today!' to which one boy simply responded, 'You smell like oranges and pizza.'

Oh. Ok.

Having consumed neither oranges nor pizza that day I was a little concerned!

In Jesus' day and age, children were at the bottom of the pecking order. They often received no education, had to work from a young age, and were excluded from many parts of life. Basically, they were unimportant, and a nuisance in the eyes of the disciples. They tried to shoo them away.

Jesus is having none of it! He tells the disciples to back off, and speaks directly to the children, letting them know that in His Kingdom, they really matter. His earlier prayer in Luke 10 shows that children often understand spiritual matters that the best adult minds in the world just don't get.

Just one more example of this 'topsy turvy' Kingdom that had everyone scratching their heads! Jesus had time for little children, even if they were annoying, loud, or said He smelt like oranges and pizza! There was, and is, no-one too 'small' for Him.

GOD FACT: God loves people that society deems 'less important', whether that's children, elderly people, drug users, people with disabilities, or 'ordinary' people like you and me! His Kingdom doors are wide open, and He won't have anyone shoo people away.

LIFE HACK: God calls us to love 'unimportant' people. Have a think of who that might be in your life. A younger (more annoying) sibling? A granny who makes you play scrabble? A classmate who is constantly left out? How could you prioritise them today?

#storytime

J esus loves a parable (a story used to illustrate a spiritual truth) and He particularly enjoys a plant-related one. Who doesn't?

So, what is it that He wants to illustrate? There are lots of nuggets stuffed into this story, but in a super slick summary, I think there are two things we can focus on today:

1)   God is at work! He is the farmer in this parable, and He goes around scattering His seed. He's not sat back on some shiny white sun lounger, sipping a Capri-Sun and watching to see how the plebs will get on. He is actively involved – more than that, He is the one sharing the Good News, using His church and people in the process.

2)   People have a choice in their response. God is a farmer, sowing seed, not a factory boss churning out robots. He scatters the seed on the ground, and there are lots of different reactions – but they come from the ground, not the farmer. This shows us that people have a choice in how they respond to the 'seed', as well as the circumstances around them. All the way through this parable, we also see the devil trying to snatch away the seed. He's trying to get people preoccupied with something else.

The crowd and the disciples found this one a tricky number to get their head around, and I don't blame them! There are a number of complex ideas going on, but Jesus wants us to see the different ways the human heart responds to His offer of salvation. He sows and lets us choose what we'll do with that seed.

GOD FACT: God is a sower, actively at work. He scatters this seed – God's Word – into the lives of many people. It doesn't matter what background you come from, many different types of people respond to God's call in faith.

LIFE HACK: Just like Jesus, we want to be sharing the Good News of the gospel! Alongside that, we need to ask Jesus to give our friends and family 'good soil' hearts. Think of one person today who you want to see respond to the Good News, and pray away!

#justkeepswimming

D o you ever feel like giving up on prayer? I know I feel like giving up on prayer all the time!

It's hard work and time-consuming, it can lead to disappointment and frustration. Sometimes I wonder if this is really worth it? Is this really achieving anything?

This parable has one clear message. KEEP GOING. KEEP SWIMMING. (Well, that second one might be from Finding Nemo, but it is pretty similar!)

We can be assured that God does hear our prayers. (Just check Psalm 65:2 if you don't believe me. See? Told you so!) But Jesus knew just how hard it can be to keep praying, particularly in the face of apparent silence or inaction. So, He gave us this story to encourage us to persevere in prayer, and not to give up when we don't see anything happen.

Now Jesus isn't telling us 'don't take no for an answer' or 'never let go of your dreams'. There will be times when the answer is 'no', and, when that's the case, we need to be willing to set that thing down and leave it be. Even when that 'no' is confusing, or difficult to accept.

Often the answer is 'wait' or 'keep going' and that is HARD. I can think of things I've prayed about for days and weeks and months and years and have yet to see any change happen. Why not throw in the towel and admit defeat? Because God's command is, 'Don't quit! Keep going!'

I used to think that God was like the judge in this story. Kinda unwilling to answer your prayers, but He might just do it if you annoyed Him enough. I was wrong about that! This story is meant to show the difference between a mean, earthly judge and our gracious, good Father. Jesus is making the point that if persistence paid off with a grumpy old dude, how much more will our merciful, loving, listening heavenly Father value it?

GOD FACT: God values persistent, bold prayer. Unless we are asking for something wrong, or He gives us a clear 'no', then His command is to keep praying and not to give up!

LIFE HACK: Think about something you've given up praying about. Ask for God's forgiveness for giving up on it and commit to 'keep going' with your prayer until you get a 'no' or a 'yes'!

#thegoodthebadandtheugly

READ LUKE 10:25-37

It's a story I'm sure you've heard before. An unfortunate soul gets an absolute doing on the side of the road to Jericho and he's pretty low on options. With no mobile phone, ambulance service, or even a wet paper towel, this guy can only hope someone will come to his aid.

This story would have been shocking to its listeners. Not just the idea that the Jewish religious leader would ignore the victim, but that an enemy Samaritan would be the one to take pity! It would have been a seriously hard pill to swallow. We see the expert in the law struggle to even name the heroic character as 'the Samaritan', so strong was his disregard for these people.

You might struggle to identify who your 'enemy' is, particularly if you don't have anyone who directly makes your life difficult. So, if that's the case, then what about this? A bit like the expert of the law, who would you struggle to see as the 'hero' in one of God's storylines? Who, in your eyes, wouldn't deserve that position? Who bugs you when they get ahead, or are doing well? Who do you think couldn't possibly be used by God in a big way, because of who they are, or what they've done? Have a think. Got someone in mind? Good! Then read on.

Remember that your eternal salvation rests entirely on the fact that God loves His enemies, and that He gives gifts to people who don't deserve them. This story absolutely shows us that we need to love our enemies, but it also teaches us that we need to be okay with God loving and exalting them too – regardless of whether we think they deserve that or not.

GOD FACT: God loves His enemies and, until you sought His forgiveness, that's what you were. He also loves to give opportunities and gifts to people who don't deserve them, demonstrating His own glory, and encouraging us to stay humble.

LIFE HACK: Who was it you thought of as undeserving of God's favour, or unusable by Him? Ask for God's forgiveness, and for an idea about how you can show that person selfless love today, just like Jesus did for you.

#finderskeepers

Read Luke 15:1-10

I
t was day one of summer camp and I'd come up with a daring game.

Me: 'So, we throw the egg around the circle, and everyone has to catch it without breaking it!'

Camper: 'Aw I've done this before. It's a trick! The egg's actually hard boiled. Nice try!!'

Next thing I knew, in an attempt to prove his hypothesis, this self-assured child had thrown the egg at my head. It was, in fact, raw. It exploded everywhere, leaving me a total mess. (Apparently, egg is good for your hair though, so maybe he was doing me a favour?)

The perpetrator was immediately apologetic, obviously worried about what I would do. He'd just thrown an egg at the Team Leader of the event… what next?! Would he lose points for his team? Get sent inside for the day? Have to wear a Humpty Dumpty costume for the remainder of the week?

None of that. Since I knew there had been no malicious intent in his eggy missile, I let him off the hook!

When we muck up, and then try and reconcile with the person we've wronged, we aren't always met with understanding and acceptance. We might not always be 'let off the hook'.

So how much worse will it be when we try and make amends with a perfect God?

These two brief parables reveal God's mind-blowing response. It isn't a punishment exercise, a grudging forgiveness, or a lecture on how 'you need to do better next time'. It's an epic celebration, a rejoicing about something precious that had got lost, and now was back where it belonged. The lamb that wandered off was quite possibly being stupid and selfish, thinking it knew better than the wise and caring shepherd but said shepherd goes out of his way to see that invaluable lamb is brought back to safety. When we repent, whether for the first time or the millionth time, God is waiting with open arms, ready to rejoice. Even one saved sinner calls for a heavenly party, because God's joy at restoring lost things goes completely off the charts.

Egg-cellent news!

GOD FACT: He is a celebratory God who throws a party every time someone turns to Him. He feels joy and relief when we come back to Him, and we don't need to fear punishment or abandonment.

LIFE HACK: Think about the day you were saved, and try to imagine the glorious uproar in heaven, the excitement and joy that you'd been brought home. Next time you feel far from God, or are worried you've wandered away, remember He still wants you just as much now as He did back then.

#branchingout

READ JOHN 12:12-19

We skip forward today to Palm Sunday, which is the start of the last week of Jesus' life on earth. It was time for the Feast of Passover, so Jesus, along with a 'great crowd', headed up to Jerusalem where it was always celebrated.

By this stage, lots of people had heard about Jesus or had seen His miracles, and listened to His teaching. They were excited to see Him arrive! They were perhaps also excited at the prospect of the Messiah coming to finally do what they'd expected all along – overthrow the Romans (who were the tyrannical rulers of the time). Perhaps Jesus had finally got His act together, gathered an army, and was ready to ride into town on an intimidating steed, ready to strike their oppressors!

But what scene do they find unfolding in its place? Crowds waving palm branches instead of swords, people calling out words of praise rather than words of war, and Jesus riding a donkey in place of a war horse.

This was no accident, nor a grand entrance gone wrong! Jesus was not only fulfilling prophecy (verse 15), He was also making a bold statement about the kind of mission He was on. In the ancient world, leaders rode horses if they were going to war, and donkeys if they came in peace.

Jesus made it clear to everyone that He was coming in peace. His target wasn't the Romans, it wasn't the Pharisees, it wasn't you or me – it was death. He was coming not to bring judgement, condemnation or war against anyone, but instead to defeat death and offer life and peace to anyone and everyone who accepted Him. Jews and Romans. Women and men. Children and adults. Rich and poor. Good and bad (and ugly!)

Jesus is the same today. He doesn't come to you riding on a war horse, bringing punishment and fear. He comes to you on a donkey, humble and gentle, on a mission of peace and rescue.

GOD FACT: God's message to us is one of life and peace because that's what He's about! His mission was to defeat death, not to defeat you.

LIFE HACK: Jesus wants us to become more like Him. Think of someone you are tempted to bring 'war' to (some form of payback) because of something they've done. Ask God to give you an idea of how you can bring peace to this person instead, following Jesus' example.

#smellysocks

READ JOHN 13:1-20

J esus knows He doesn't have long left on earth. What would I have done with my remaining hours if I was in His shoes? Swim with dolphins? Skydive? Trip to Disneyworld? (Or the Disney store at least!)

Unsurprisingly, it was none of the above.

Jesus wants to spend every last minute He has with His friends, serving them, and preparing them to live without His physical presence. He didn't demand a big party, give a rousing speech, or remind them all who was boss. Instead, He got down on His knees and washed their feet.

Don't forget that in those days there were no showers, no socks, no aloe-vera-cleansing-and-moisturising-scented-foot-cream...just sweaty feet that walked along dusty roads in smelly sandals.

It was a dirty, humiliating job normally assigned to a lowly servant. And Jesus, who knew He had come from God and had complete power over everything (verse 3) was the one doing it. He wanted the disciples to understand that His love for them (and us) was so great, there was nothing He wouldn't stoop to. There was nothing too dirty, nothing too embarrassing or ugly about them (and us!) that He wouldn't get down on His knees and deal with.

Jesus makes it plain. If He, the Son of God, was willing to do that kind of thing, then we had better be willing too!

Verse 15 says, 'I have set the example, and you should do for each other exactly what I have done for you.'

Now, to be clear, Jesus doesn't mean that He wants us to go out on a literal feet-washing mission! He is asking us to do exactly what He did in humbling Himself and serving others. There should be no job that is too 'low' for us, whether it's stacking chairs after church, feeding our messy baby brother, or befriending that person at school who just doesn't fit in. If the Creator and Sustainer of the whole universe wasn't 'too good' for the unglamorous, unspectacular and (sometimes) unpleasant job of serving others, then we definitely can't claim to be!

GOD FACT: Even though Jesus had no obligation to, He humbled Himself and didn't think He was too important for ANY task.

LIFE HACK: Think of one unglamorous job in your household that no-one is in a rush to do. (Maybe taking the bins out, cleaning the bathroom, or mowing the grass.) Then, quietly go and do it. Not for recognition or reward, but because Jesus humbled Himself for you and He wants you to follow in His footsteps.

#suppertime

READ LUKE 22:7-23

It's time for Passover. (Sorry, whatover?) Passover! This was a festival reminding the Israelites of their escape from Egypt, and how the blood of the Passover lamb had saved them from the Angel of Death. (Not familiar with this story? Give it a read in Exodus 12.) God had commanded them to celebrate this festival every year, so they would remember the great way God had delivered them.

So this meal is no pot-luck dinner, take-away night, or Taco Tuesday! To these men, this meal is already deeply significant. They would have eaten it remembering what God had done, and looking forward to His promise to, one day, send a Messiah and rescue them again.

A promise Jesus wanted them to see was about to be delivered.

Jesus breaks the bread as a sign of how His body will be broken for them.

Jesus drinks the wine and tells them of how His blood will be spilt for them.

He also tells them it's a sign of the 'new covenant', replacing the old law-and-sacrifice-heavy covenant God had given to Moses back in the day.

I'm sure the disciples knew something very important was going on, but they didn't really get it at the time. We have the benefit of understanding what Jesus was going to do, and has now done.

His broken body and spilt blood mean a new covenant that we can enjoy. It's not one of meticulous rule keeping, and an endless cycle of sacrifice, but one of totally undeserved grace and freedom.

Jesus tells His disciples to keep this practice up in remembrance of Him. Today, we call this Communion. Communion isn't about feeling really guilty about all the ways we've slipped up, and it's not a 'magic formula' that brings us forgiveness. Neither is it something that only 'super Christians' can partake in. Communion is all about refreshing your mind, remembering God's overwhelming love for us and His humility in being willing to be broken for you and me. It's about celebrating the new covenant of grace, one that brings a total forgiveness of sin and a life-giving friendship with God. It's a reminder that it's not about what you do, it's about what He's done!

GOD FACT: Jesus gave up everything, even His very life, in order to bring about a new covenant that offers us all the opportunity to be made a new creation. A covenant that lets us find our identity in Christ and not in our own behaviours.

LIFE HACK: If you've put your trust in Jesus then follow His command to take part in Communion! Don't focus on your own failings and the opinions of others, but fix your eyes on Jesus and His perfect sacrifice, given in love.

#endingsandbeginnings

We skip forward today to Jesus' arrest. Talk about people doing a 180! On Palm Sunday, the crowds had been shouting Jesus' name in praise, and now they are baying for His blood!

Jesus' own friend betrays Him. He's publicly arrested and dragged away. All His   friends scatter, bar one who ultimately pretends not to know Him. Jesus is beaten, mocked and insulted, and worse is still to come.

How do you react in a situation where you've been treated unfairly, or are falsely accused? I'll tell you what I do, I argue! Defend myself! Name and shame the real perpetrator!

Does Jesus do any of these things? No. He doesn't.

In fact, amidst the evil, the violence, and the abandonment, He steps in to heal the ear of someone on the enemy side. Someone who was playing an active part in His coming crucifixion. Even in the worst moments of His life, Jesus' focus was still on serving and loving His enemies and not on defending Himself.

In the times you feel like you've really let God down, or have actively gone against Him, remember that in both His life and death, Jesus was all about reaching out and bringing healing – whether it was to an ear on a servant, or forgiveness to a sinful soul. Because of His death on the cross, Jesus doesn't rush to bring punishment but instead, intervenes to bring healing to our hearts when we ask Him.

GOD FACT: God steps in to heal broken things. Because He chose the cross instead of defending Himself, we can rest assured He will heal our spiritual brokenness when we bring it to Him.

LIFE HACK: Think of something in your life that needs God's help and healing. Perhaps it's an attitude to a family member, a wrong relationship, or a bad promise you've made. Whatever it is, bring it to Him now. Ask Him to bring about change!

#itstoolate

It seems like everything has gone wrong. In this dark chapter, it feels like there is only evil and destruction. But when we keep our eyes on Jesus, and listen to the words He says, we see Him bringing life, even in the midst of such horror.

Two criminals are being crucified at the same time as Jesus, but they have very different ideas about what's really going on. The first one sends a barrage of insults Jesus' way – using up his last reserves of energy to continue to reject God up until the very end.

The second one, however, has a different perspective in the ebbing moments of his life. He recognises his own guilt, understands Jesus' worth, and asks for a chance to be part of the coming Kingdom. It's a request Jesus answers.

Jesus takes His last breath, and the two thieves die soon after, meaning that the thief on the cross was probably the first person to be saved after Jesus' death. But hold on, why was he the first? He's not exactly a poster boy for Jesus' Kingdom, is he?

In fact, he is! This man had lived an evil, selfish life; he'd rejected God right up until the very end. But in his dying moments, when it was waaaaaaaaaaaaay too late to start 'living right' or 'making up for the past', he is ushered into God's Kingdom. Jesus showed that His suffering on the cross was exactly for highly unlikely candidates like this criminal, who had no chance of ever being 'good enough'.

Jesus fully paid this man's debt on that cross and once a debt has been paid, it disappears! There was nothing more for the newest member of God's family to do, and nothing for him to fear.

GOD FACT: Jesus paid it all on the cross and, as such, God's Kingdom is not about good behaviour and earning brownie points! The thief could do absolutely nothing to absolve, or make up for, his past but it still wasn't too late for him. It's never too late for anyone in this life.

LIFE HACK: Thank Jesus that, because of His life and death, there is nothing you can do to make God love you more, and nothing you can do to make God love you less! Pray for one person for whom you are tempted to feel like it's 'too late' for, asking God to give you boldness and opportunities to share this totally amazing truth with them!

#daythree

READ LUKE 24:1-12

It's tempting to think of the cross as the epitome of Jesus' ministry, but wait! What about the bit when He rises from the dead, blowing everyone's minds?!?

It's hard to imagine just how these women felt. They would have been completely crushed, heart-broken and distraught. Their world had come crashing down, and they were suddenly alone. Jesus was dead. It was all over. Or was it?

They arrive at the tomb to find some puzzling goings-on:

1. The body has gone. (Wait, what? How?)

2. The stone has been rolled away. (Remember it was a huge stone. Probably would've been easier to roll away an elephant)

3. Two mad-shiny guys have appeared. (AKA angels.)

4. These angels tell the women not to look for the living among the dead. (e.g. Jesus is alive you dafties!)

Suddenly, the whole thing is flipped on its head, and their grief is turned to joy. 'Yes!' they might have said to one another. 'This is what Jesus said! He told us this would happen! He's really alive! C'mon, let's go tell the team!!'

Can you imagine the joy? The celebration? The smiles, the laughter, and the sheer elation at this turn of events? These women probably didn't understand the wonderful implications of their news, certainly not in the way that we do now, but their joy was still abundant.

There never has been, and never will be, greater news or anything more worthy of celebration. Not just for Jesus' mates back in the day, but for us, today and now! He is risen, defeating death and freeing us forever from its grip!

GOD FACT: Jesus triumphed over death! His resurrection is the best news these women, and the whole world, could have ever received! He is alive!

LIFE HACK: If you haven't put your trust in Jesus then think about why that might be. Ask God to give you a full understanding of what He has done, like He did for these women. The same Spirit that raised Jesus from the dead is in those who trust in Him, so if you do trust in Jesus ask God to give you joy simply because Jesus is alive again. Listen to Tim Hughes' song 'Happy Day' and celebrate!

#intrusionofconfusion

W e're not sure why these two chaps were heading to Emmaus. Perhaps they wanted to try and clear their heads, maybe they were worried that Jerusalem was unsafe, or possibly they were doing a sponsored walk to raise funds for their local donkey sanctuary. Who knows!

The writer doesn't think it's important for us to know, but Luke does want us to see that Cleopas and his pal had reaaaaally not grasped what Jesus had done. That they were walking away from Jerusalem in confusion and grief, truly believing it was all over.

Not for long! Jesus steps in and, although initially they don't recognise Him, by the end of the day they finally understand who He really is, and what His plan was all along.

What strikes me here is how Jesus was the one putting in all the effort! He is the one who takes the initiative, who reaches out to His hopeless friends; even though they are moving away from Him (both literally and spiritually), and from the truth.

Just like in His parables, we see again that Jesus is all about going after people. So often we see that He is the proactive one, bringing comfort and understanding to His friends.

GOD FACT: God loves us with a love that is active and working! He doesn't leave us struggling on our own with confusion and doubt, but steps in to help at the right time.

LIFE HACK: It can be easy to think about our spiritual life as being all the things we 'do' (reading, praying, church, etc.) Although these are all good things, don't forget that God is relentlessly pursuing you! Talk to Him about something you have confusion or doubt about, then spend some time waiting, allowing Him the opportunity to minister to you.

#nowyouseehim

LUKE 24:36-53

Jesus' time on earth is complete, and He is about to leave His disciples for the final time, before returning to the Father. Before He goes (and after a fishy snack), He commissions them:

Verses 47-48 say, 'So beginning in Jerusalem, you must tell everything that has happened.'

This group of men and women are witnesses to Jesus' life, death, and resurrection, so now He commands them to share what they've seen and experienced. They have a transformative, life-bringing message of liberation from guilt, sin, and death. They have something to really shout about!

That means we do too! Although we weren't there to see and hear these things first hand, through the Word of God and through our own experiences, we too are witnesses of God's amazing grace. Likewise, we are given the same commission by Jesus to make disciples. As we live our lives, whether it's at school, at work, hanging out with friends, or at church, we are to be encouraging and growing our Christian brothers and sisters, but also sharing God's love and message of salvation with those who don't know Him yet.

Jesus left earth that day, but one day He'll be coming back! Not to heal people, to preach on the street, or to hang on a cross but to bring His new, perfect, super-fun, sin-and-sadness-free Kingdom; and He wants us to partner with Him in handing out the invites.

GOD FACT: Jesus is coming back to bring a new Kingdom that will be beyond our wildest dreams. He wants us to work with Him in sharing His Good News for this life and the next!

LIFE HACK: Think of one person you'd like to talk to about Jesus today, and ask God for a really obvious opportunity, His help, and a good dose of courage to do just that!

With that, you've completed the fifty-day-God-fact-and-life-hack-Bible-challenge (snappy description much?)!

But don't stop now!

I hope you've seen how great it is to learn more about God, and how practical His Word can be in directing our lives.

God's Word is a life-giving treasure trove, which we've barely dipped our toes into (like, maybe only half-way up the toenail of the teeny one). Your last challenge is to make a daily plan to read God's Word, listening to what He has to say to you through it. It could be with a parent or friend, using Bible reading notes, or an app. The choice is up to you!

Keep reading, keep listening, keep applying and, of course, keep using ridiculously long hash-tags. #becauseeveryonelovesah ashtagwhethertheyadmititornotbecausetheyarebrilliantokbye

You Asked
by William Edgar

It can be difficult to ask questions, far less answer them. Perhaps you've felt that sometimes the questions you really want to ask just can't be answered. They're too difficult; too embarrassing; and perhaps you shouldn't be asking them anyway. William Edgar takes a selection of twenty-four questions just like that – questions that are asked by young adults just like you – and gives a biblical, common sense, unpatronising answer to each. Edgar tackles issues such as 'Where is God?' 'Can we trust the Bible?' 'What about love and sex?' 'Does God love gay people?' 'When will the world end?' 'Are there vampires?' 'Can I have real friends?'

ISBN: 978-1-78191-143-3

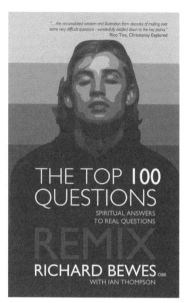

THE TOP **100** QUESTIONS

SPIRITUAL ANSWERS TO REAL QUESTIONS

REMIX

RICHARD BEWESOBE

WITH IAN THOMPSON

The Top 100 Questions Remix
by Richard Bewes with Ian Thompson

As a popular media broadcaster and conference speaker, Richard Bewes often faces tricky questions about the Christian faith. This book collects answers to the top 100 asked by people from all opinions and religious beliefs – remixed for young people.

These are not 'pat' answers to make you feel smug and the questioner seem stupid – they are the sort of thing you could use in a conversation – if only you had thought it out in time!

When you socialise with friends or course mates, living out the Christian faith in the 21st century naturally attracts questions. Here is some instant experience to stop you slapping your head and saying, 'If only I'd said that!'

The Top 100 Questions Remix – it's a great way to answer your mates' questions and help you explain why you are a Christian.

ISBN: 978-1-84550-191-4

CHRISTIAN FOCUS PUBLICATIONS

Christian Focus   Christian Heritage   CF4K   Mentor

Christian Focus Publications publishes books for adults and children under its four main imprints: Christian Focus, CF4K, Mentor and Christian Heritage. Our books reflect our conviction that God's Word is reliable and Jesus is the way to know him, and live for ever with him.

Our children's publication list includes a Sunday school curriculum that covers pre-school to early teens, and puzzle and activity books. We also publish personal and family devotional titles, biographies and inspirational stories that children will love.

If you are looking for quality Bible teaching for children then we have an excellent range of Bible stories and age-specific theological books.

From pre-school board books to teenage apologetics, we have it covered!

Find us at our web page:
www.christianfocus.com

CF4 •K
Because you're never
too young to know Jesus